# GRIDDLING

**Quarto.com**



First Published in 2026 by The Harvard Common Press, an imprint of The Quarto Group,
100 Cummings Center, Suite 265-D, Beverly, MA 01915, USA.
T (978) 282-9590 F (978) 283-2742

EEA Representation, WTS Tax d.o.o.,
Žanova ulica 3, 4000 Kranj, Slovenia.
www.wts-tax.si



The Harvard Common Press titles are also available at discount for retail, wholesale, promotional, and bulk purchase. For details, contact the Special Sales Manager by email at specialsales@quarto.com or by mail at The Quarto Group, Attn: Special Sales Manager, 100 Cummings Center, Suite 265-D, Beverly, MA 01915, USA.

30 29 28 27 26 1 2 3 4 5

ISBN: 978-1-57715-654-3

Digital edition published in 2026
eISBN: 978-1-57715-655-0

Library of Congress Cataloging-in-Publication Data

Names: Harvard Common Press editor
Title: Griddling
Description: Beverly, MA, USA : Harvard Common Press, an imprint of The Quarto Group, 2026. | Series: Great cooking outdoors | Includes index.
Identifiers: LCCN 2025026382 (print) | LCCN 2025026383 (ebook) | ISBN 9781577156543 hardcover | ISBN 9781577156550 ebook
Subjects: LCSH: Barbecuing | Skillet cooking | Outdoor cooking | LCGFT: Cookbooks
Classification: LCC TX840.B3 G744 2026 (print) | LCC TX840.B3 (ebook) | DDC 641.5/78--dc23/eng/20250702
LC record available at https://lccn.loc.gov/2025026382
LC ebook record available at https://lccn.loc.gov/2025026383

The content in this book was previously published in *The Epic Outdoor Griddle Cookbook* by Adam and Brett Walton (Harvard Common Press, 2022) and *Smashed* by Adam and Brett Walton (Harvard Common Press, 2023)

Design and Page Layout: Megan Jones Design
Photography: Leigh Olson Photography, with styling by Jenelle Olson Plunkett: 17, 18, 22, 25, 32, 35, 36, 39, 40, 43, 44, 46, 57, 61, 62, 65, 90, 93, 94, 97, 98, 101, 105, 106, 109, 110, 113, 114, 117, 118, 121, 122; Michelle Miller Photography: 28, 49, 50, 53, 54, 58, 69, 70, 73, 74, 77, 78, 81, 82, 85, 86, 89; Shutterstock: 7, 9, 12, 14, 21, 29, 30, 66, 103
Illustration: Michael Korfhage

Printed in Guangdong, China TT102025

GREAT COOKING OUTDOORS

# GRIDDLING

EDITORS OF THE HARVARD COMMON PRESS

HARVARD COMMON PRESS

# CONTENTS

# INTRODUCTION: GRIDDLING BASICS

Congratulations on your new griddle. Welcome to a sizzling new way to cook outdoors! The recipes in this book are your guide to mastering the art of griddle cooking—whether you're flipping pancakes at sunrise, searing burgers at sunset, or crafting delicious appetizers and meals in between. With its wide, flat surface and even heat distribution, the outdoor griddle opens up endless possibilities for flavorful, fun meals. Inside, you'll find 50 mouthwatering recipes, plus some helpful tips to get you started—all designed to make your next griddle meal easy, enjoyable, and tasty. So, fire up the griddle and let's get cooking!

## TOOLS

Here is a list of the tools you can use regularly and how they can help you get the most out of your griddle experience.

**Dome:** A basting dome is a great tool to help create steam or just raise the temperature of a specific area on a griddle. This helps when you are cooking other foods on the griddle but still need to melt the cheese on your burger. Placing the dome over the burger does not disrupt the cooking process or affect the temperature on other areas of the grill.

**Large tray or bucket:** Because most griddle cooks happen a bit more quickly than grill cooks do, you may find you don't have time to run into the house for something you forgot. Having a large tray or bucket to carry out all necessary items for your cook is the answer.

**Press:** These are known as a bacon press or grill press. There are also now specific "burger" presses.

**Scraper-chopper:** There's just something about holding a spatula in one hand and the scraping tool in the other that helps give you total control of every cook! Investing in a regular scraper and a smaller food-grade "paint" scraper (wood handle slant-edge scraper) is best.

**Spatulas of all sizes:** A large spatula keeps food together when turning, moving, or flipping better than a thin, lightweight spatula will. Speaking of thinner spatulas, these are perfect, though, for a hibachi cook, or any cook where you need to keep your hands moving! Because they are lighter, your hands will be thankful that they aren't lugging the large spatula around the griddle surface.

**Squeeze bottles:** Squeeze bottles are easy to grab and super convenient for holding different oils, sauces, and dressings. You can also have one dedicated to water for steaming on the griddle.

**Tongs:** Just like a good spatula, the right tongs are ideal for every griddle cook. The long handle is perfect for reaching over the hot griddle surface.

**Warming rack:** Because the griddle can accommodate a large amount of food at one time, a warming rack is the perfect place to move foods off direct heat while a cook is still happening. It's also the perfect place to cook biscuits right on the griddle top.

### Other Items You Might Find Helpful

**Batter dispenser:** It's hard to find a quality one, but a batter dispenser, primarily for pancakes, is a great tool to have to make uniform pancakes that cook evenly.

**Disposable grease trays:** Nearly all griddle manufacturers make disposable grease trays. They are inexpensive but make the cleanup process so much easier.

**Griddle soft cover:** The greatest way to preserve your griddle for long-term use is to have a soft, water-resistant cover to protect it.

**Paper towels:** Having paper towels ready at all times is extremely handy—so much so that many griddles even come with a paper towel holder now.

**Shakers:** Look for the larger aluminum salt and pepper (or other seasoning) shakers that can dispense larger amounts of seasoning, which can come in handy when cooking on the griddle.

**Taco rack:** A must-have for taco cooks! This rack also works great for holding hot dogs and sandwiches!

## PANTRY STAPLES: SPICES

Everyone has their favorite spices for their burgers! Whether it earned favorite status back in the day because it was a family staple or you just discovered an amazing combination last week, these burgers and sandwiches are the perfect vehicles.

That said, you can't go wrong with just salt and pepper! Here are some spices you may want to keep stocked in your pantry:

- salt
- pepper
- garlic powder
- onion powder
- adobo seasoning
- paprika
- chipotle powder
- hot sauce

## PANTRY STAPLES: OILS

Any cooking oil, whether it be vegetable oil, avocado oil, or even beef tallow, works well, so don't hesitate to use your favorite! For smash burgers, however, it is best to steer clear of olive oil, as it has a lower smoke point and can burn at a higher temperature.

## GRIDDLE TEMPERATURES

Cooking on a griddle is similar to cooking on a stovetop. The following temperature ranges are approximate. Use them to guide your cooking.

| | | |
|---|---|---|
| **Low** | 250°F–320°F | 121°C–160°C |
| **Medium-Low** | 320°F–340°F | 160°C–171°C |
| **Medium** | 340°F–410°F | 171°C–210°C |
| **Medium-High** | 410°F–430°F | 210°C–221°C |
| **High** | 430°F–500°F | 221°C–260°C |

## COOKING TEMPERATURES FOR MEATS AND EGGS

|  |  |
|---|---|
| **Burgers and Ground Beef** | 375°F–425°F (190°C–218°C) |
| **Steaks** | 425°F–475°F (218°C–246°C) |
| **Chicken** | 375°F–400°F (190°C–204°C) |
| **Pork Chops and Ribs** | 425°F–450°F (218°C–232°C) |
| **Pork Tenderloin** | 375°F–425°F (190°C–218°C) |
| **Hot Dogs** | 350°F–400°F (176°C–204°C) |
| **Sausages** | 375°F–425°F (190°C–218°C) |
| **Fish Fillets or Fish Steaks** | 350°F–400°F (176°C–204°C) |
| **Shrimp and Scallops** | 375°F–425°F (190°C–218°C) |
| **Eggs** | 300°F–350°F (176°C–204°C) |

Consult your griddle's owner's manual for guidance on which knob settings create these temperatures.

| COOKING TEMPERATURES FOR VEGETABLES | |
|---|---|
| **Asparagus** | 350°F–400°F (176°C–204°C) |
| **Bell Peppers** | 375°F–425°F (190°C–218°C) |
| **Broccoli** | 375°F–425°F (190°C–218°C) |
| **Brussels Sprouts** | 375°F–425°F (190°C–218°C) |
| **Corn** | 350°F–400°F (176°C–204°C) |
| **Mushrooms** | 350°F–400°F (176°C–204°C) |
| **Onions** | 375°F–425°F (190°C–218°C) |
| **Potatoes (Chopped or Diced)** | 375°F–425°F (190°C–218°C) |
| **Potatoes (Frozen French Fries)** | 375°F–425°F (190°C–218°C) |
| **Squash and Zucchini** | 350°F–400°F (176°C–204°C) |

Consult your griddle's owner's manual for guidance on which knob settings create these temperatures.

# 1

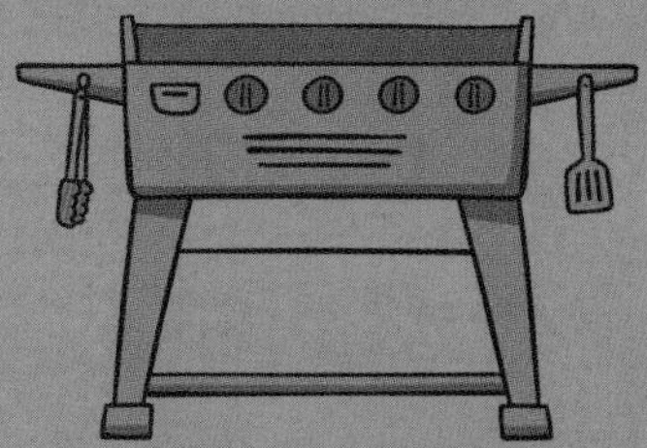

# BREAKFASTS

# PERFECT SCRAMBLED EGGS

**YIELD:** 2 to 4 servings

**One thing that you MUST be able to cook on the griddle is scrambled eggs. These are the best scrambled eggs you'll ever eat—breakfast, lunch, or dinner. A garnish, like a dash of hot sauce or spoonful of salsa, makes them even better.**

4 large eggs

1½ teaspoons salt

1½ teaspoons freshly ground black pepper

1 tablespoon (14 g) unsalted butter

**1.** Bring the griddle to low heat.

**2.** In a medium-size bowl, whisk the eggs, salt, and pepper until well mixed.

**3.** Place the butter on the griddle to melt, spreading it out in the area where you'll cook the eggs. Slowly pour the eggs onto the griddle to make sure they don't run everywhere. As the mixture starts to cook underneath, gently fold in the sides. Continue to cook and fold the eggs for 30 to 45 seconds until fluffy and golden. Remove from the griddle and serve.

**TIP**

For a heartier breakfast, add some well-chopped precooked salami, summer sausage, or ham to the griddle right after you add the eggs.

# GRILLED CHEESE BREAKFAST BURRITOS

4 tablespoons (60 ml) vegetable oil, divided

6 thick-cut bacon slices

1 pound (454 g) ground mild sausage

4 to 6 large eggs

½ teaspoon salt

½ teaspoon freshly ground black pepper

2 to 4 tablespoons (28 to 56 g) unsalted butter

1 (3-ounce [85 g]) can Hatch green chiles

1 cup (115 g) shredded Mexican-style cheese blend

2 cups (230 g) shredded cheddar cheese

4 (10-inch [25 cm]) burrito-size flour tortillas

Salsa for dipping

Hot sauce for dipping

**YIELD:** 4 servings

**Adding cheese to the outside of this burrito puts it over the top. It's everything you love—eggs, fillings, and all—with loads of cheese.**

**1.** Bring the griddle to medium-low heat. Pour 2 tablespoons (30 ml) of oil onto the griddle and let it heat until you see a wisp of white smoke.

**2.** Place the bacon in the hot oil and cook, turning, until crispy. Remove and chop into small bits.

**3.** Pour the remaining 2 tablespoons (30 ml) of oil onto the griddle and place the sausage on top. Cook the sausage until browned and no longer pink, then remove from the griddle to a bowl.

**4.** In a medium-size bowl, whisk the eggs, salt, and pepper to combine.

**5.** Place the butter on the griddle to melt, spreading it out in the area where you'll cook the eggs. Slowly pour the eggs onto the griddle. As the mixture starts to cook underneath, gently fold in the sides. Continue to cook until fluffy and golden.

**6.** Pour the can of green chiles onto the eggs, add the bacon, sausage, and Mexican-style cheese blend. Cook, mixing it all together, until the cheese melts. Transfer the egg mixture to a large bowl or plate.

**7.** Place one tortilla on a clean work surface. Place a large spoonful of the eggs in the middle of the tortilla. Fold in the sides first, then from the edge closest to you, pull the tortilla over the ingredients and finish rolling the burrito. Repeat with the remaining tortillas and eggs.

**8.** Lay down a strip of shredded cheddar on the griddle, the length of a burrito, and place the first burrito directly onto the cheese. Cook for 30 to 45 seconds, then place another strip of shredded cheddar directly in front of the burrito. Using a scraper or spatula, start to roll the burrito from the back, making sure the cheese sticks to the tortilla, and roll it onto the front strip of cheddar. Cook for 30 to 45 seconds, then carefully pull the burrito off the griddle. Repeat this process with each burrito. Serve with salsa and hot sauce for dipping.

# BREAKFAST TACOS WITH CHORIZO AND EGGS

**YIELD:** 4 servings

**Most breakfast tacos combine scrambled eggs with some kind of meat, thereby providing a two-fisted protein fix for the start of a busy day. Beef, such as leftover barbecued brisket, and pork, in the form of carnitas, bacon, or pork sausage, are the most common meats. Spicy chorizo sausage is a favorite in Texas and in the Southwestern US.**

8 eggs

2 ounces (4 tablespoons [55 g]) unsalted butter, cut into 2 even pieces

¾ pound (340 g) uncooked chorizo sausage

Salt

8 warm medium to large flour tortillas

4 ounces (115 g) shredded sharp cheddar (about 1 cup)

1 large avocado, peeled and thinly sliced

Tomato or tomatillo salsa for serving

**1.** Bring the griddle to medium-low heat. In a medium-size bowl, lightly beat the eggs. Melt one of the butter pieces on the griddle until it is bubbling hot.

**2.** Place the chorizo on top of the melted butter and cook it, stirring often, until it is golden brown and cooked through, about 8 minutes. Remove the chorizo with a slotted spatula to a bowl.

**3.** Add the remaining butter piece to the griddle surface and heat it until it is bubbling hot. Cook the eggs in the butter until they are scrambled but not dry, 3 to 4 minutes. Season to taste with salt. Return the chorizo to the griddle and stir to combine it evenly with the eggs.

**4.** Arrange the tortillas on individual plates. Divide the egg mixture between the tortillas and top each with shredded cheese and avocado slices. Serve immediately with the salsa on the side.

# BREAKFAST CREPES

- 1 cup (120 g) all-purpose flour
- ¾ cup (180 ml) whole milk
- ½ cup (120 ml) water
- 3 tablespoons (45 ml) melted unsalted butter, plus more for cooking
- 2 large eggs
- 1 tablespoon (12.5 g) sugar
- 1½ teaspoons vanilla extract
- Pinch of salt
- Filling of choice for serving

**YIELD:** 4 to 6 crepes

**The light and fluffy flavor and texture of crepes are unforgettable, and the ease with which these cook on the griddle makes them a no-brainer for breakfast. Serve with your favorite fillings, such as fresh bananas, blueberries, raspberries, or strawberries, and top with a drizzle of caramel sauce, chocolate syrup, or honey, and a dusting of powdered sugar.**

**1.** In a medium-size bowl, whisk the flour, milk, water, melted butter, eggs, sugar, vanilla, and salt until smooth. Cover and refrigerate for at least 1 hour.

**2.** Bring the griddle to medium heat.

**3.** Place 1 tablespoon (14 g) of butter on the griddle to melt. Pour one ladleful of batter onto the melted butter, then use a clean dowel, in a circular motion, to flatten the batter. Once flat, lift and flip the crepe to cook the second side—no more than 30 seconds per side. Repeat with the remaining batter, adding more butter as needed.

**4.** To fill the crepes: Place the crepes on a work surface. Put your filling into the center of the crepe and gently fold each side over the filling.

# EGGNOG FRENCH TOAST

**YIELD:** 4 slices

**If you are looking for a holiday tradition, may we suggest this eggnog French toast? Serve with your favorite toppings.**

1 cup (240 ml) eggnog

2 large eggs

1 tablespoon (14 g) unsalted butter

4 slices artisan bread (such as brioche)

**1.** In a shallow bowl, whisk the eggnog and eggs until fully combined.

**2.** Bring the griddle to medium-low heat.

**3.** Place the butter on the griddle to melt. One at a time, dredge the bread slices in the eggnog wash and place it in the melted butter. Cook for 1 to 2 minutes until browning begins. Flip the bread and cook for 1 to 2 minutes more, or until browned.

### TIP

Aside from syrup and extra butter, some other things you can serve alongside the French toast are cinnamon, honey, whipped cream, fruit preserves, and chopped fresh berries.

### FRENCH TOAST

1 cup (235 ml) milk

2 teaspoons sugar

½ teaspoon vanilla extract

2 to 3 large eggs

1 tablespoon (14 g) butter

4 slices white bread

### MONTE CRISTO SANDWICHES

4 slices Swiss cheese

¼ pound (115 g) deli sliced turkey breast

¼ pound (115 g) deli sliced ham

2 tablespoons (16 g) powdered sugar

Raspberry jam for serving

# PRESSED MONTE CRISTO FRENCH TOAST SANDWICH

**YIELD:** 2 sandwiches

**Have you ever had a Monte Cristo sandwich? This French toast version is as good, or maybe even better, than the original, and it's so simple to make! Note: A heavy cast iron or other large grill/griddle press is best suited for use with this sandwich.**

**1.** In a medium-size bowl, mix the milk, sugar, vanilla, and eggs until fully combined.

**2.** Bring the griddle to medium-low heat.

**3.** Once the griddle is to temperature, lay down a pat of butter and move it around in a circle until fully melted on the surface. Dredge the bread in the egg wash and place it on the melted butter. Cook for approximately 1 to 2 minutes until it begins to brown. Flip the bread and cook for 1 to 2 minutes more, or until browned.

**4.** Once the French toast is flipped, place a slice of Swiss cheese on each slice of French toast. Evenly divide the sliced turkey and ham and place each stack on 2 of the French toast slices. Top the stacks with the remaining slices of French toast. Place a grill/griddle press on top of the sandwiches and hold for 1 minute.

**5.** Carefully flip the sandwiches and repeat the same cooking process on the second side by pressing lightly until the cheese is melted through, ensuring you do not burn the outside of the French toast.

**6.** Once pulled and plated, lightly sprinkle the powdered sugar over each sandwich and serve with a side of raspberry jam (for dipping the sandwich in).

# EVERYTHING BAGEL BREAKFAST SMASH

**YIELD:** 1 bagel sandwich

**"Yup, this one's happening today!" Now introducing the Everything Bagel Breakfast Smash! Note: A heavy cast iron or other large grill/griddle press is best suited for use with this sandwich. You'll also need parchment paper.**

2 slices bacon

1 everything bagel

1 tablespoon (14 g) butter

4 to 5 ounces (115 to 140 g) ground sausage, formed into a loosely packed meatball

1 slice American cheese

1 egg

½ teaspoon salt

½ teaspoon freshly ground black pepper

**1.** Bring the griddle to medium heat.

**2.** While the griddle is warming, place the strips of bacon on the griddle. (Placing the bacon on the griddle before it is hot helps keep the bacon from curling too much.)

**3.** Cook the first side until browned and flip. Continue to cook until the bacon is done to the desired crispiness. Pull and place on a paper towel–lined plate to drain off excess grease.

**4.** Cut the bagel open, butter the insides, and place on the griddle for 30 seconds to 1 minute until light brown and lightly crispy. Set aside.

**5.** Once the griddle is to temperature, place the sausage meatball on the griddle. Cook for about 30 seconds. After 30 seconds, place a piece of parchment paper on top and press down with a grill/griddle press and hold for 10 to 15 seconds.

**6.** Flip the sausage patty over. Place the American cheese on top and let it start to melt. After 30 seconds to 1 minute, pull the patty and place it on the bottom bagel. Break up and place the bacon on top of the patty.

**7.** Clear the excess sausage scrap and collect the leftover grease or lay down a pat of butter for your egg. Cook the egg over easy. Once the egg white becomes opaque, carefully flip the egg and add salt and pepper. After 30 to 45 seconds, pull the egg and place it on top of the bacon. Top with the remaining bagel half.

- 2 cups (450 g) leftover mashed potatoes
- 2 eggs
- ¼ cup (31 g) all-purpose flour
- ¼ cup (40 g) diced yellow onion
- 2 to 3 chives, diced
- ¼ cup (30 g) shredded cheddar cheese
- 2 tablespoons (28 ml) vegetable oil
- Sour cream for serving (optional)

# MASHED POTATO CAKES

**YIELD:** 5 to 6 cakes

**Leftover mashed potatoes get a second life in these crispy, golden-brown potato cakes. They're the perfect blend of soft interior and crunchy edges. Serve them for breakfast, brunch, or as a cozy side dish—no one will guess they started as leftovers.**

**1.** In a medium-size bowl, combine the mashed potatoes, eggs, flour, onion, chives, and cheese until evenly mixed.

**2.** Bring the griddle to medium heat.

**3.** Once the griddle is to temperature, pour the oil on the griddle and scoop ½ cup (113 g) of the mixture onto the griddle, repeating until the mixture is all gone.

**4.** Cook for about 3 to 4 minutes on the first side or until golden brown.

**5.** Flip and lightly press and continue to cook until the second side is golden brown. (The potato cakes should resemble cooked pancakes.)

**6.** Serve with some sour cream or your favorite condiment.

2

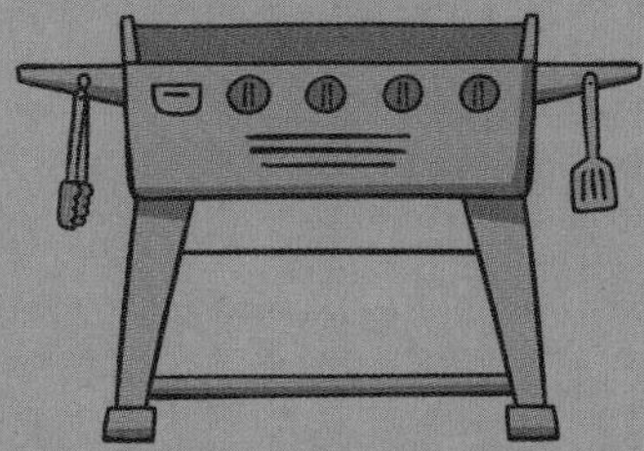

# APPETIZERS AND SIDES

# CHEESESTEAK EGG ROLLS

**YIELD:** 8 to 10 medium-size egg rolls

**Want to impress your family and friends with what might be the "star" appetizer at the next big gathering? This. Is. IT! This recipe may need to be doubled, or even tripled, to satisfy the crowd.**

6 to 8 tablespoons (90 to 120 ml) vegetable oil, divided

2 tablespoons (28 g) unsalted butter

1 large yellow onion, diced

1 green bell pepper, diced

2 teaspoons salt, divided

2 teaspoons freshly ground black pepper, divided

1 pound (454 g) rib eye, shaved or sliced as thinly as possible

8 to 10 egg roll wrappers

10 slices provolone cheese

½ cup (120 ml) water

Favorite dipping sauce for serving

**1.** Bring the griddle to medium-low heat.

**2.** Pour 1 tablespoon (15 ml) of oil onto the griddle, then place the butter in it to melt. Lay the onion in the melted butter, followed by the green pepper and add 1 teaspoon of salt and 1 teaspoon of pepper. Cook for 5 to 6 minutes, moving the vegetables slowly, until the onion begins to turn translucent. Set the vegetables aside in a bowl.

**3.** Pour 3 to 4 tablespoons (45 to 60 ml) of oil onto the griddle. Place the rib eye flat in the hot oil, spreading it out, and season with the remaining salt and pepper. Cook for 1 to 2 minutes to create a sear. Once the meat begins to turn brown, stir and chop the rib eye with a scraper to break up the meat. Mix in the onion and pepper and set aside.

**4.** Place 1 egg roll wrapper on a work surface in a "diamond" shape, with one corner aimed down (this helps with the rolling and folding process). In the middle of the wrapper, place a spoonful of the steak and vegetables, then place 1 slice of provolone over the steak, folding it to fit. Fold the bottom corner of the egg roll wrapper up and over the meat and cheese, then fold in each side of the wrapper, tucking them tightly while not breaking the wrapper. Once the sides are folded (like an envelope), continue to roll the egg roll, leaving just the top inch (2.5 cm) exposed. Dip your finger in the water and run it along the exposed edge of the wrapper to help "seal" the egg roll. Repeat with the remaining ingredients.

**5.** If needed, pour the remaining 2 to 3 tablespoons (30 to 45 ml) of oil onto the griddle and place the egg rolls in the oil. Cook for 1 to 2 minutes until the bottoms are golden brown. Flip each egg roll and continue to cook, turning as necessary, until all sides are golden brown. If the ends need to be crisped, hold the egg rolls with tongs so they stand on end. Pull the egg rolls off the griddle and slice diagonally from one corner to the other. Serve with your favorite dipping sauce.

½ cup (120 g) Mexican crema

½ cup (120 g) mayonnaise

½ cup (8 g) minced fresh cilantro

2 tablespoons (30 ml) freshly squeezed lime juice

2 teaspoons grated lime zest

1 garlic clove, minced

8 medium-size ears sweet corn, husked

2 tablespoons (30 ml) vegetable oil

½ cup (60 g) crumbled Cotija cheese

1 teaspoon ground chipotle pepper

# MEXICAN STREET CORN (ELOTES)

**YIELD:** 8 servings

**Yes, it really tastes as good as it looks! The smoky chipotle pepper brings all the flavors together, making you wonder why you ever ate corn on the cob any other way.**

**1.** In a medium-size bowl, whisk the crema, mayo, cilantro, lime juice, lime zest, and garlic until blended. Refrigerate until needed.

**2.** Bring the griddle to medium-low heat.

**3.** Pour the oil onto the griddle and place the corn in the oil. Cook the corn for 15 to 20 minutes, rotating it every 2 minutes to ensure it does not burn, and cooking until your desired doneness is achieved (medium-brown color on the softened corn kernels. (Alternatively, add 2 to 3 tablespoons [30 to 45 ml] of water, close the hood or place a dome on the corn, and steam for about 15 minutes, turning the corn every 2 minutes, until done.)

**4.** Pull the corn off the griddle and let cool for 3 minutes. Using a basting brush or a spoon, lather each ear of corn entirely with the crema mixture. Sprinkle all sides with Cotija cheese and season with chipotle pepper to taste.

# FRIED PICKLE CHIPS

**YIELD:** 6 to 8 servings

**These homemade fried pickles really are as good, if not better, than any restaurant dish anywhere. Serve with your favorite dipping sauce!**

1 (32-ounce [905 g]) jar dill hamburger pickle chips

2 cups (240 g) all-purpose flour

1 to 2 tablespoons (12 to 24 g) Usual Suspects Seasoning (page 92)

1 to 2 teaspoons paprika

2 cups (480 ml) buttermilk

2 to 3 tablespoons (30 to 45 ml) vegetable oil

**1.** Pour the pickles into a colander in the sink to drain. Rinse with cold water, drain again, and pat dry with paper towels.

**2.** In a large bowl, whisk the flour, Usual Suspects Seasoning to taste, and paprika to taste. Pour the buttermilk into a separate shallow bowl. One by one, coat each pickle chip in the flour mixture, dip it into the buttermilk, then back into the flour mixture to coat completely. Place the coated pickles on a plate, then bring the plate to the griddle.

**3.** Bring the griddle to medium-low heat.

**4.** Pour the oil onto the griddle and let heat until you see a wisp of white smoke. Place the coated pickles in the oil and cook for 3 to 4 minutes until the bottoms begin to turn golden brown. Flip the pickles and cook for 3 to 4 minutes until the second side is also golden brown. Pull the pickles off the griddle and let cool for 2 to 3 minutes before serving.

- Vegetable oil for frying
- 1 cup (240 ml) milk
- 2 large eggs
- 2 tablespoons (25 g) granulated sugar
- 1 teaspoon vanilla extract
- 2 cups (240 g) all-purpose flour
- 1 teaspoon baking powder
- ¼ teaspoon salt
- Powdered sugar for serving

# STATE FAIR FUNNEL CAKES

**YIELD:** 8 to 10 large funnel cakes

**This recipe is definitely worthy of a blue ribbon! Once you figure out how to use an aluminum pan on the griddle surface safely, these cakes will be a breeze to make.**

**1.** Bring the griddle to medium-high heat.

**2.** Place a 15.75 × 11.25-inch (39 × 28 cm) aluminum foil pan on the griddle and fill it with about 2 inches (5 cm) of oil. Bring the oil to between 365°F and 375°F (185°C and 190.5°C).

**3.** While the oil comes to temperature, in a large bowl, whisk the milk, eggs, granulated sugar, and vanilla until well mixed. In a medium-size bowl, whisk the flour, baking powder, and salt to combine. Add the dry ingredients to the wet ingredients and whisk until evenly mixed with no clumps. Transfer the batter to a pouring pitcher, or use a plastic bag with a small to medium-size hole cut out of a bottom corner (keep the hole covered until you are ready to pour the batter into the oil).

**4.** In a circular motion, pour the batter into the hot oil, ensuring the batter lays over itself as it cooks, forming a 6-inch (15 cm) cake. Fry the cake for 1 to 2 minutes until golden brown. Flip the cake and cook for 1 to 2 minutes until the second side is golden brown. Transfer the funnel cake to a paper towel to drain. Sprinkle with powdered sugar while hot and serve. Repeat with the remaining batter.

# PINEAPPLE COLESLAW

**YIELD:** 4 servings

**Try this slaw on tacos or burgers or as a standalone side. The possibilities are endless.**

1 (12-ounce [340 g]) bag broccoli slaw mix

½ pineapple, peeled, cored, and diced, juice reserved

1 cup (240 g) mayonnaise

1 tablespoon (15 ml) rice vinegar

1 teaspoon ground white pepper

½ teaspoon salt

**1.** In a large bowl, combine the broccoli slaw and pineapple.

**2.** In a small bowl, whisk the mayonnaise, vinegar, reserved pineapple juice, white pepper, and salt until smooth. Pour the sauce over the broccoli mixture and toss to coat evenly. Refrigerate for 4 to 6 hours, or overnight for the best flavor. Toss before serving.

### TIP

For some spice and heat, whisk in 1 tablespoon (15 g) of finely minced jalapeño (hot), serrano (medium), or Anaheim (mild) chile peppers when you make the dressing.

# HAWAIIAN MACARONI SALAD

**YIELD:** 4 to 6 servings

**No Hawaiian plate lunch is complete without the amazing macaroni salad and white rice on the side! As the perfect side dish with Hawaiian Barbecue Chicken (page 96), or as a stand-alone meal, this salad is perfection!**

- 1 pound (454 g) elbow macaroni
- 6 tablespoons (90 ml) apple cider vinegar
- 3 teaspoons (18 g) salt, divided
- 1 cup (240 ml) whole milk, plus more as needed
- 6 tablespoons (75 g) sugar
- 2 cups (480 g) mayonnaise, divided
- ½ cup (80 g) grated or minced white onion
- 2 cups (220 g) grated carrot
- 1 teaspoon ground white pepper
- 4 scallions, white and green parts, thinly sliced

**1.** Cook the macaroni according to the package directions. Drain and transfer to a large bowl. While the pasta is still hot, stir in the vinegar and set aside to cool.

**2.** In a small bowl, stir together 1½ teaspoons (9 g) of salt, the milk, sugar, and 1 cup (240 g) of mayonnaise until blended. Add the mayo mixture to the still slightly warm macaroni and mix until well coated. Cover and refrigerate for 1 hour, or up to 4 hours, until fully cooled.

**3.** To the cooled macaroni, add the remaining 1 cup (240 g) of mayonnaise, the onion, and carrot. Gently stir to coat and combine. If the pasta appears a bit dry, add up to ½ cup (120 ml) more milk. Season with the remaining 1½ teaspoons (9 g) of salt and the white pepper. Garnish with the scallions to serve.

# 3

# SANDWICHES

# "CLASSIC" ITALIAN PANINI

**YIELD:** 1 sandwich

**Feel free to dress the sandwich to your liking or keep it classic. Note: A heavy cast iron or other large grill/griddle press is best suited for use with this sandwich.**

1 tablespoon (14 g) unsalted butter

1 small ciabatta bread, split in half

2 slices provolone cheese

2 slices deli sliced Black Forest Ham

2 slices deli sliced genoa salami

2 slices deli sliced roasted turkey breast

Sliced tomato, for topping

Shredded lettuce, for topping

Red onion, thinly sliced, for topping

Banana peppers, sliced, for topping

1 tablespoon (15 ml) Italian dressing

Salt and freshly ground black pepper

Dill pickle spear for serving (optional)

---

**1.** Bring the griddle to medium-low heat.

**2.** While the griddle is coming up to temperature, spread the butter on the inside sides of the ciabatta bread.

**3.** Lay the bread butter-side down on the griddle.

**4.** Once the bread is lightly browned, pull the top slice of bread and set it aside. Turn the bottom slice over and begin building the sandwich in the following order: provolone cheese, ham, salami, turkey breast, tomato, lettuce, onion, banana peppers, Italian dressing, salt and pepper to taste, top half of the ciabatta bread.

**5.** Place a large grill/griddle press on top of the sandwich. You do not need to apply pressure if using a cast iron press. Let sit for 2 to 3 minutes or until the bottom slice of bread is golden brown.

**6.** Carefully flip the sandwich, lay the press again, and repeat the same cooking process on the second side (about 2 additional minutes).

**7.** Pull from the griddle, slice, and add a pickle spear on the side before serving.

½ tablespoon (7.5 ml) olive oil

1 (10-ounce [280 g]) bag of fresh spinach leaves

1 tablespoon (14 g) unsalted butter

2 slices sourdough bread

2 slices Swiss cheese

4 slices vine-ripened tomatoes

½ teaspoon salt

½ teaspoon freshly ground black pepper

6 to 8 slices fresh avocado

1 tablespoon (14 g) mayonnaise

# CHEESY VEGETARIAN PRESSED SANDWICH

**YIELD:** 1 sandwich

**Simple and fresh, this pressed vegetarian option is more filling than you'd think! It's so packed with flavor, it's destined to become the new healthier selection in your recipe rotation. Note: A heavy cast iron or other large grill/griddle press is best suited for use with this sandwich.**

**1.** Bring the griddle to medium-low heat.

**2.** Once the griddle is to temperature, pour the oil on the griddle, then add the spinach.

**3.** Cook the spinach in the oil, moving the spinach around, for approximately 2 minutes (the spinach will reduce by more than half the original size). Pull from the heat and set aside in a bowl.

**4.** Melt butter on the griddle and move it around in a circle until fully melted on the surface. Place the slices of bread in the melted butter.

**5.** On 1 slice of bread, place the 2 slices of Swiss cheese, followed by the spinach, tomatoes, salt, pepper, and the avocado.

**6.** On the second slice of bread, spread the mayonnaise, then place it mayonnaise-side down on top of the sandwich.

**7.** Place a grill/griddle press on top of the sandwich and cook for about 1 minute or until the bottom slice of bread is golden brown and the cheese begins to melt.

**8.** Carefully flip the sandwich and repeat the same cooking process on the second side.

**9.** Pull from the heat and cut in half before serving.

# CLASSIC TURKEY CLUB PANINI

**YIELD:** 1 sandwich

**A delicious turkey club? In a panini press? Delectable! Note: A heavy cast iron or other large grill/griddle press is best suited for use with this sandwich.**

2 slices bacon

1 tablespoon (14 g) butter

2 slices white bread

2 slices deli sliced turkey breast

1 tomato slice

½ teaspoon salt

½ teaspoon freshly ground black pepper

1 slice Swiss cheese

**1.** Bring the griddle to medium-low heat.

**2.** While the griddle is warming, place the strips of bacon on the griddle. (Placing the bacon on the griddle before it is hot helps keep the bacon from curling too much.) Cook the first side until browned and flip.

**3.** Continue to cook until the bacon is done to the desired crispiness. Pull and place on a paper towel–lined plate to drain off excess grease.

**4.** Bring the griddle up to medium heat.

**5.** Once the griddle is to temperature, lay down a pat of butter and move it around in a circle until fully melted on the surface.

**6.** Place 1 of the slices of bread on the melted butter, followed by the turkey breast, bacon, and tomato. Once the tomato is placed, sprinkle with salt and pepper, lay the Swiss cheese on top, and place the second slice of bread. Place a grill/griddle press on top of the sandwich, without putting pressure on it.

**7.** After the bottom slice of bread is golden brown, lay down another pat of butter and flip the sandwich over. Place the grill/griddle press back on top of the sandwich.

**8.** Once the bottom slice of bread is golden brown, pull the sandwich.

1 tablespoon (14 g) unsalted butter

2 slices marbled rye bread

1 tablespoon (14 g) mayonnaise

1 tablespoon (11 g) yellow mustard

4 slices Swiss cheese

5 to 6 slices deli pastrami

# PRESSED PASTRAMI ON RYE STACKS

**YIELD:** 1 sandwich

**Who would have thought that simply stacking hot pastrami and Swiss cheese on rye bread would be this good? Note: A heavy cast iron or other large grill/griddle press is best suited for use with this sandwich.**

**1.** Bring the griddle to medium-low heat.

**2.** Once the griddle is to temperature, butter 1 side of each slice of the marbled rye and place 1 of the buttered slices of bread on the griddle. Spread ½ tablespoon (7 g) of mayonnaise and ½ tablespoon (5.5 g) of mustard on the bread and add 2 slices of Swiss cheese.

**3.** While the bread is toasting, place the pastrami on the griddle and cook each side for 20 to 30 seconds to get it hot. Place the pastrami on top of the Swiss cheese and top with 2 more slices of Swiss cheese. Spread the remaining mustard and mayonnaise on the other slice of bread (non-buttered side) and place it on top of the pastrami, butter-side up.

**4.** Once the bottom slice of bread is toasted to a golden brown, carefully flip and place a grill/griddle press on top of the sandwich and press and hold for about 1 minute. (You could also use a large spatula.) Continue cooking until the second side is golden brown and the cheese is completely melted.

# PASTRAMI PATTY MELTS

**YIELD:** 2 servings

**It's not often that a small "addition" makes such a profound impact, but the pastrami here busts that misconception. And although you might be able to eat a patty melt all day, every day, this cook with the addition of pastrami? Next. Level. BOOM!**

11 ounces (308 g) 80/20 ground beef

5 dashes Worcestershire sauce

Salt and freshly ground black pepper

2 tablespoons (28 g) unsalted butter, plus more for toasting the bread

½ medium-size yellow onion, sliced

2 tablespoons (30 ml) vegetable oil

4 ounces (115 g) shaved pastrami

4 slices Swiss cheese

4 slices rye bread

2 tablespoons (30 g) Thousand Island dressing

**1.** In a medium-size bowl, combine the ground beef, Worcestershire sauce, and salt and pepper to taste. Mix, ensuring the ingredients are combined well. Divide the ground beef into two equal portions and form each into a ball.

**2.** Bring the griddle to medium heat.

**3.** Use 1 tablespoon (14 g) of butter to coat a small area of the griddle and place the onion on it. Cook the onion until it begins to caramelize, then add the remaining 1 tablespoon (14 g) of butter to the onion. Cook until the onion becomes translucent, then move the onion to a cooler area of the griddle, not over direct heat.

**4.** Adjust the griddle heat to medium-high heat.

**5.** Use 2 tablespoons (30 ml) of oil to coat the middle of the griddle. Put the meatballs in the oil, ensuring enough space between them that they don't smash together. Using a burger press, firmly press one burger down onto the griddle, holding the press for 10 seconds. Repeat with other burger. Cook for about 1 minute to create a sear, then flip the burgers.

**6.** Place the pastrami on the griddle to heat up, moving it constantly until it is hot. Divide the pastrami between the burgers, then top the pastrami with Swiss cheese and let the cheese melt.

**7.** To toast the bread, coat one side of each rye slice with butter. Place two pieces of bread, butter-side down, on the griddle. Top with Thousand Island dressing. Place the burger patties on the bread, then top with onion and the other slice of bread, butter-side up (put mayonnaise on both sides of the top piece of bread to toast it and add extra flavor to the patty melt). Cook until the bottom bread is toasted, carefully flip the entire sandwich, and toast the top side. Pull the sandwiches off the griddle and let cool slightly before serving.

2 tablespoons (28 g) unsalted butter, divided

½ yellow onion, sliced

½ pound (225 g) deli sliced roast beef

4 slices Swiss cheese

2 French baguettes, sliced

½ cup (120 ml) prepared au jus

# PRESSED FRENCH DIP SANDWICH

**YIELD:** 2 sandwiches

**You may be one of those people who, whenever you go to a restaurant that serves a French dip sandwich, can't NOT order it. Learning how to make a simple version of your own might be one of the best cooking decisions you've ever made. Note: A heavy cast iron or other large grill/griddle press is best suited for use with this sandwich.**

**1.** Bring the griddle to medium-low heat.

**2.** Once the griddle is to temperature, melt 1 tablespoon (14 g) of butter on the griddle, then add the onions. Sauté the onions in the butter until they become translucent (about 5 to 6 minutes) and move them to a cooler area of the griddle, not over direct heat.

**3.** Place the roast beef in single layers on the griddle to lightly brown, approximately 30 seconds, and flip. Cook for 30 more seconds and then pile the roast beef into 2 even stacks and place 2 slices of Swiss cheese on each stack.

**4.** Place half of the onions on each of the stacks and place each stack into a baguette. Melt the remaining butter on the griddle by moving it around in a circle on the surface. Place each sandwich on the melted butter and place a grill/griddle press on top. Press for about 1 minute and carefully flip the sandwiches and press again.

**5.** Pull once each side is lightly browned. Serve with the side of au jus.

# NASHVILLE HOT CHICKEN SANDWICHES

**YIELD:** 2 servings

**Until you've had a Nashville hot chicken sandwich, you just don't know!**

### BRINE

2 to 3 cups (480 to 720 ml) buttermilk

1 cup (240 ml) pickle brine

Usual Suspects Seasoning (page 92) for seasoning

2 boneless, skinless chicken thighs

### SAUCE

2 tablespoons (10 g) cayenne pepper

1½ tablespoons (23 g) brown sugar, plus more as needed

½ teaspoon chili powder

½ teaspoon garlic powder

½ cup (120 ml) vegetable oil

### DREDGE

2 cups (240 g) all-purpose flour

2 tablespoons (24 g) Usual Suspects Seasoning (page 92)

1 tablespoon (7 g) paprika

2 to 3 teaspoons vegetable oil

Mayonnaise for serving

Kaiser rolls for serving

Sandwich pickles for serving (preferably Claussen)

---

**1.** To make the brine: In a shallow dish, whisk the buttermilk, pickle brine, and Usual Suspects Seasoning to taste until blended. Add the chicken thighs and turn them to coat in the brine. Cover and refrigerate for at least 1 hour, or up to 3 hours.

**2.** To make the sauce: While the chicken marinates, in a small bowl, whisk the sauce ingredients to combine and set aside. The sauce may separate, so whisk again occasionally.

**3.** To make the dredge: In a shallow bowl, stir together the flour, Usual Suspects Seasoning, and paprika to blend.

**4.** Bring the griddle to medium-low heat.

**5.** Pour 2 to 3 tablespoons (30 to 45 ml) of oil onto the griddle and let heat until you see a wisp of white smoke. Remove the chicken from the brine and dredge it in the flour mix to completely coat, then place the chicken in the hot oil. Discard the brine. Cook for about 2 minutes, or until the bottom side is golden brown. Flip the chicken and cook the other side for about 2 minutes until golden brown. Continue flipping and cooking the chicken until the internal temperature reaches at least 165°F (74°C).

**6.** Pull the cooked chicken off the griddle and place it on paper towels or a cooling rack to drain. Whisk the sauce and coat the chicken with it, ensuring full coverage.

**7.** To assemble: Spread mayo on the cut sides of the rolls. Place a piece of chicken on the bottom roll, top with two pickle slices, and add the top roll.

# SWEET STICKY BUFFALO SANDWICHES

**YIELD:** 2 servings

**Looking for a creative way to change up your buffalo chicken game? The sauce can be used for all things chicken-fried! Note: The aluminum pan used for frying is thin and punctures easily. Add the oil while the pan is on the griddle, and avoid using knives or tongs in the pan.**

### SWEET STICKY BUFFALO SAUCE

1½ cups (338 g) packed light brown sugar

6 tablespoons (90 ml) Frank's RedHot Original Cayenne Pepper Sauce

¼ cup (60 ml) water

### SWEET STICKY BUFFALO SANDWICH

Vegetable oil for frying

2 to 3 cups (240 to 360 g) all-purpose flour

Salt and freshly ground black pepper

1 cup (240 ml) buttermilk

1 large boneless, skinless chicken breast, halved horizontally

2 kaiser rolls, split

Mayonnaise for serving

Ranch or blue cheese dressing for serving

Sandwich pickles for serving

**1.** To make the buffalo sauce: In a medium-size saucepan over medium-low heat on the stovetop or griddle, whisk the brown sugar, hot sauce, and water to combine. Cook, stirring occasionally, until the brown sugar is dissolved. Set aside for dipping and basting.

**2.** To make the buffalo sandwich: Bring the griddle to medium-high heat.

**3.** Place a 15.75 × 11.25-inch (39 × 28 cm) aluminum foil pan on the griddle over high heat and fill it half full of oil. Bring the oil to between 325°F and 345°F (163°C and 174°C). If it gets hotter than this, bring the temperature down. You do not want to burn the breading on the chicken before the meat is cooked through.

**4.** Place the flour in a shallow bowl and season with salt and pepper. Whisk to combine. Place the buttermilk in another shallow bowl. One piece at a time, coat the chicken in the buttermilk, then dredge in the seasoned flour, ensuring the entire breast is covered (including any cracks; it helps to press the flour into the chicken). Shake off any excess flour and gently place the chicken in the hot oil. Fry for 1 to 2 minutes, flip the chicken, and cook until the breading is a light golden brown color (it will continue to darken after being pulled from the oil). Check the internal temperature of the chicken to ensure it is at least 165°F (74°C). Baste the hot chicken with the sticky buffalo sauce.

**5.** To build the sandwiches: Put the rolls on plates, cut-side up, and spread both halves with mayo. Top the bottom bun with a piece of chicken, then a dab of ranch, some pickle slices, and finish with the top bun. Pass the extra sauce for dipping.

# CUBAN SANDWICHES

**YIELD:** 4 servings

**Layers of roast pork, ham, Swiss cheese, pickles, and mustard are tucked into soft Cuban bread, then pressed until warm and crisp. It's a timeless favorite—rich in flavor, history, and tradition. Update your recipe book with this one to create a crispy, not overly hard sandwich with a flavor that impresses everyone!**

8 slices deli ham

2 tablespoons (22g) yellow mustard

4 Cuban rolls, halved horizontally

1 pound (454 g) cooked Cuban-Style Marinated Pork, shredded

8 slices Swiss cheese

Pickle chips for the sandwiches and serving

**1.** Bring the griddle to medium-low heat.

**2.** Place the ham on the griddle, heating each side for 30 seconds to 1 minute.

**3.** Spread a thin layer of mustard on the insides of the Cuban rolls. Layer a generous amount of pork on the bottom half of the roll. Place two slices of ham on the pork on each sandwich, followed by two slices of Swiss cheese. Top each sandwich with pickle chips (as many or as few as you like). Place the top roll on the sandwiches and place the sandwiches on the griddle. Using a press or a sturdy spatula, press down firmly on each sandwich, holding the press for 2 to 3 minutes, or until the bottom roll is toasted. Gently flip the sandwich and continue the process. The sandwich will flatten considerably as it is pressed. Slice the sandwich diagonally, nearly corner to corner, and serve!

# CUBAN-STYLE MARINATED PORK

**YIELD:** 8 to 10 servings

½ cup (120 ml) freshly squeezed orange juice

½ cup (120 ml) freshly squeezed lime juice

7 garlic cloves, minced

2 tablespoons (30 ml) extra-virgin olive oil

1½ teaspoons salt

1 teaspoon ground cumin

1 teaspoon dried oregano

⅛ teaspoon freshly ground black pepper

1 (3-pound [1.3 kg]) boneless pork shoulder roast

**1.** In a gallon (3.8 L)-size or larger resealable plastic bag, combine the orange and lime juices, garlic, oil, salt, cumin, oregano, and pepper. Add the roast, seal the bag, and turn the bag to coat the pork. Refrigerate for at least 6 hours to marinate and up to 24 hours.

**2.** Remove the pork from the marinade and place it in a slow cooker. Discard the marinade. Cover and cook on medium-low heat for 5 to 7 hours, or until the pork is fork-tender and falls apart easily.

4

# SMASH BURGERS

# SMASH BURGER ROYALE

**YIELD:** 1 burger

**If you ever wondered if an egg belongs on a burger, this one answers that question . . . yes, yes it does! It'll make you ask yourself why you haven't been doing this all along.**

1 tablespoon (15 ml) vegetable oil

1 large egg

2½ teaspoons salt, divided

2½ teaspoons freshly ground black pepper, divided

6 to 7 ounces (170 to 200 g) 80/20 ground beef, divided into 2 loose meatballs

2 slices American cheese

1 potato hamburger bun

Ketchup for topping

Mustard for topping

Mayonnaise for topping

4 dill pickle chips

Shredded lettuce for topping

Sliced tomato for topping

½ red onion, thinly sliced

Additional 1 tablespoon (14 g) mayonnaise, for toasting the buns (optional)

---

**1.** Bring the griddle to medium-high/high heat. Once the griddle is to temperature, pour the oil on the griddle.

**2.** Crack the egg on the griddle surface. Wait until the white is completely opaque to gently flip the egg, season with ½ teaspoon each of salt and pepper, and pull from the surface after 30 seconds to a minute, trying not to break the yolk.

**3.** Place the 2 meatballs in the oil, ensuring space between the meatballs to give them room to be smashed. Sprinkle salt and pepper liberally onto the meatballs.

**4.** After about 30 seconds, smash each meatball all the way down flat with a burger smasher or the back side of the spatula, using the back side of another spatula to help apply pressure. Hold the smash down for 10 to 15 seconds.

**5.** Once each burger is smashed and you see the juices begin to rise to the surface, use the spatula and quickly flip them and place a slice of American cheese on each burger.

**6.** Pull each burger from the heat.

**7.** Place the burgers, stacking one on top of the other, on the bottom bun. Build in the following order (optional): bottom bun, swirl of ketchup, swirl of mustard, swirl of mayonnaise, pickle chips, smash burger patties, egg, lettuce, tomato, onion, top bun.

- 1 tablespoon (15 ml) vegetable oil
- 12 ounces (340 g) 80/20 ground beef, divided into four 3-ounce (85 g) loosely packed meatballs
- 1 packet (1 ounce [28 g]) taco seasoning
- 1 cup (225 g) shredded Mexican cheese blend
- 2 hamburger buns (preferably potato buns)
- 1 tomato, sliced
- 1 cup (43 g) shredded lettuce
- ½ cup (124 g) nacho cheese sauce
- 2 tablespoons (28 ml) taco sauce

# TACO SMASH BURGER

**YIELD:** 2 burgers

**When your family wants smash burgers, but it's "Taco Tuesday," this recipe will make everyone happy.**

**1.** Bring the griddle to medium-high heat. Once the griddle is to temperature, pour the oil on the griddle.

**2.** Place the 4 meatballs in the oil, ensuring space between the meatballs to give them room to be smashed. Sprinkle the taco seasoning liberally on the meatballs.

**3.** After about 30 seconds, smash each meatball all the way down flat with a burger smasher or the back side of the spatula, using the back side of another spatula to help apply pressure. Hold the smash down for 10 to 15 seconds.

**4.** Once each burger is smashed and you see the juices begin to rise to the surface, use the spatula and quickly flip them and place a handful of shredded Mexican cheese on each burger.

**5.** Pull each burger from the heat.

**6.** Place the burgers, stacking one on top of the other, on the bottom buns. Build in the following order: bottom bun, smash burger patties, tomato, lettuce, nacho cheese sauce, taco sauce, top bun.

# MUSHROOM & SWISS SMASH BURGER

**YIELD:** 1 burger

**Once you try this simple and decadent recipe, it might just become an instant classic—not just for you, but for your family as well!**

**MUSHROOM GRAVY**

4 tablespoons (55 g) butter, separated

2 tablespoons (16 g) all-purpose flour

2 cups (475 ml) beef stock, or beef broth

3 cups (210 g) sliced baby bella mushrooms

½ teaspoon salt

¼ teaspoon freshly ground black pepper

½ teaspoon Worcestershire Sauce

½ teaspoon soy sauce

**BURGERS**

1 tablespoon (15 ml) vegetable oil

6 to 7 ounces (170 to 200 g) 80/20 ground beef, divided into two 3- to 3½-ounce (85 to 100 g) loosely packed meatballs

2 teaspoons salt

2 teaspoons freshly ground black pepper

2 slices Swiss cheese

1 potato hamburger bun

Mushroom Gravy (See above)

1 tablespoon (14 g) mayonnaise, for toasting the buns (optional)

**1.** To make the gravy: In a medium saucepan over medium heat on the griddle, melt 2 tablespoons (28 g) of butter and slowly add the flour, mixing until a paste is created. Slowly stir in the beef stock or broth.

**2.** While the gravy is cooking and thickening, melt 2 more tablespoons (28 g) of butter on the griddle over medium-low heat, place the mushrooms in the butter, and add the salt and pepper.

**3.** While the mushrooms are sautéing, add Worcestershire sauce and soy sauce to the gravy. Once the mushrooms are softened, pull from the heat.

**4.** As the gravy comes to a boil, lower the heat and add the mushrooms.

**5.** Continue cooking for 4 to 5 minutes or until the sauce is thickened.

**6.** To make the burgers: Bring the griddle to medium-high/high heat. Once the griddle is to temperature, pour the oil on the griddle.

**7.** Place the 2 meatballs in the oil, ensuring space between the meatballs to give them room to be smashed. Sprinkle salt and pepper liberally on the meatballs.

**8.** After about 30 seconds, smash each meatball all the way down flat with a burger smasher or the back side of the spatula, using the back side of another spatula to help apply pressure. Hold the smash down for 10 to 15 seconds.

**9.** Once each burger is smashed and you see the juices begin to rise to the surface, use the spatula and quickly flip them and top with cheese.

**10.** Pull each burger from the heat.

**11.** Place the burgers, stacking one on top of the other, on the bottom bun. Top with a generous spoonful of the Mushroom Gravy and place the top bun.

# TEXAS BBQ SMASH BURGER

**YIELD:** 2 burgers

**If you aren't from Texas, it won't matter because you'll fully understand the sentiment behind the saying "Don't mess with Texas!"**

2 tablespoons (28 g) unsalted butter

4 slices Texas toast bread

1 tablespoon (15 ml) vegetable oil

12 ounces (340 g) 80/20 ground beef, divided into four 3-ounce (85 g) loosely packed meatballs

2 teaspoons salt

2 teaspoons freshly ground black pepper

4 slices Monterey Jack cheese, or cheese of your choice

1 tablespoon (14 g) mayonnaise

4 large fried onion rings

Texas-style BBQ sauce, for topping

**1.** Bring the griddle to medium-high/high heat.

**2.** While the griddle is coming up to temperature, spread butter on both sides of each slice of the Texas toast bread and place on the griddle. Cook until they are a light golden brown and then flip. Once the other sides are a light golden brown, pull and set aside.

**3.** Once the griddle is to temperature, pour the oil on the griddle.

**4.** Place the 4 meatballs in the oil, ensuring space between the meatballs to give them room to be smashed. Sprinkle salt and pepper liberally on the meatballs.

**5.** After about 30 seconds, smash each meatball all the way down flat with a burger smasher or the back side of the spatula, using the back side of another spatula to help apply pressure. Hold the smash down for 10 to 15 seconds.

**6.** Once each burger is smashed and you see the juices begin to rise to the surface, use the spatula and quickly flip them and place a slice of Monterey Jack cheese on each burger.

**7.** Pull each burger from the heat.

**8.** Place the burgers, stacking one on top of the other, on the bottom slices of Texas toast. Build in the following order: bottom bread, swirl of mayonnaise, smash burger patties, onion rings, Texas BBQ sauce. Add a swirl of mayonnaise on the inside of the top slice of Texas toast and place on top of the burger.

# CALIFORNIA SMASH BURGER WITH AVOCADO, BACON, AND RANCH

**YIELD:** 1 burger

**This is West Coast comfort food in burger form. It's crunchy, creamy, salty, and tangy in every bite. Basically, it tastes like sunshine and good decisions.**

1 tablespoon (15 ml) vegetable oil

6 to 7 ounces (170 to 200 g) 80/20 ground beef, divided into two 3- to 3½-ounce (85 to 100 g) loosely packed meatballs

2 teaspoons salt

2 teaspoons freshly ground black pepper

2 slices Swiss cheese

1 potato hamburger bun

½ tablespoon (7 g) mayonnaise

2 slices cooked bacon

2 tomato slices

1 small avocado, thinly sliced

½ red onion, thinly sliced

Ranch dressing, for topping

Additional 1 tablespoon (14 g) mayonnaise, for toasting the buns (optional)

**1.** Bring the griddle to medium-high/high heat.

**2.** If toasting the buns: While the griddle is coming up to temperature, spread the mayonnaise on the inside of the top and bottom buns and lay them on the griddle facedown. Pull the buns when they are a light golden brown and set aside.

**3.** Once the griddle is to temperature, pour the oil on the griddle.

**4.** Place the 2 meatballs in the oil, ensuring space between the meatballs to give them room to be smashed. Sprinkle salt and pepper liberally on the meatballs.

**5.** After about 30 seconds, smash each meatball all the way down flat with a burger smasher or the back side of the spatula, using the back side of another spatula to help apply pressure. Hold the smash down for 10 to 15 seconds.

**6.** Once each burger is smashed and you see the juices begin to rise to the surface, use the spatula and quickly flip them and place a slice of Swiss cheese on each burger.

**7.** Pull each burger from the heat.

**8.** Place the burgers, stacking one on top of the other, on the bottom bun. Build in the following order: bottom bun, mayonnaise, smash burger patties, bacon, tomatoes, avocado, additional pinch of salt and pepper, onion, ranch dressing. Add another spread of mayonnaise on the top bun and place on top of the burger.

# CHILI CHEESE SMASH BURGER

**YIELD:** 1 burger

**While chili may be associated with fall and winter seasons, to be able to enjoy it all year long, why not place your chili of choice on a cheesed smash burger? Boom! Meet your new year-round pick.**

- 1 tablespoon (15 ml) vegetable oil
- 6 ounces (170 g) 80/20 ground beef, divided into two 3-ounce (85 g) loosely packed meatballs
- 2 teaspoons salt
- 2 teaspoons freshly ground black pepper
- 2 slices American cheese
- 1 potato hamburger bun
- ½ cup (124 g) chili, heated
- ½ cup (58 g) shredded cheddar cheese
- ½ red onion, thinly sliced

**1.** Bring the griddle to medium-high/high heat. Once the griddle is to temperature, pour the oil on the griddle.

**2.** Place the 2 meatballs in the oil, ensuring space between the meatballs to give them room to be smashed. Sprinkle salt and pepper liberally on the meatballs.

**3.** After about 30 seconds, smash each meatball all the way down flat with a burger smasher or the back side of the spatula, using the back side of another spatula to help apply pressure. Hold the smash down for 10 to 15 seconds.

**4.** Once each burger is smashed and you see the juices begin to rise to the surface, use the spatula and quickly flip them and place a slice of America cheese on each burger.

**5.** Pull each burger from the heat.

**6.** Place the burgers, stacking one on top of the other, on the bottom bun. Place the chili on top of the burger, followed by the shredded cheddar cheese and onion. Place the top bun on the burger.

# CHEDDAR ON RYE SMASH BURGER

**YIELD:** 1 burger

**There's something about the combination of cheddar cheese on rye bread that just works so well together. Add 80/20 ground beef smashed into the perfect burger, and you've got one of the heartiest smash burgers there is!**

1 tablespoon (14 g) unsalted butter

2 slices rye bread

1 tablespoon (15 ml) vegetable oil

6 to 7 ounces (170 to 200 g) 80/20 ground beef, divided into two 3- to 3½-ounce (85 to 100 g) loosely packed meatballs

2 teaspoons salt

2 teaspoons freshly ground black pepper

2 slices cheddar cheese

Mustard for topping

Mayonnaise for topping

4 dill pickle chips

Shredded lettuce for topping

½ red onion, thinly sliced

1 tomato, sliced

**1.** Bring the griddle to medium-high/high heat.

**2.** While the griddle is coming up to temperature, spread the butter on 1 side of each slice of bread and lay them butter-side down on the griddle. Once the bread is toasted to a light golden brown, pull and set aside.

**3.** Once the griddle is to temperature, pour the oil on the griddle.

**4.** Place the 2 meatballs in the oil, ensuring space between the meatballs to give them room to be smashed. Sprinkle salt and pepper liberally on the meatballs.

**5.** After about 30 seconds, smash each meatball all the way down flat with a burger smasher or the back side of the spatula, using the back side of another spatula to help apply pressure. Hold the smash down for 10 to 15 seconds.

**6.** Once each burger is smashed and you see the juices begin to rise to the surface, use the spatula and quickly flip them and place a slice of cheddar cheese on each burger.

**7.** Pull each burger from the heat.

**8.** Place the burgers, stacking one on top of the other, on the bottom slice of bread. Build in the following order (optional): bottom slice of bread, swirl of mustard, swirl of mayonnaise, smash burger patties, pickle chips, lettuce, onion, tomato, top slice of bread.

1 tablespoon (14 g) mayonnaise

2 potato hamburger buns

1 tablespoon (15 ml) vegetable oil

12 ounces (340 g) ground chicken, divided into four 3-ounce (85 g) loosely packed meatballs

4 teaspoons (14 g) Usual Suspects Seasoning (page 92)

4 slices Swiss cheese

4 slices deli sliced honey ham

2 tablespoons (30 g) honey mustard

Additional mayonnaise, for topping (optional)

# CHICKEN CORDON BLEU SMASH BURGER

**YIELD:** 2 burgers

**The perfect balance of chicken, ham, Swiss cheese, and honey mustard will guarantee that this becomes your new favorite way to Cordon Bleu. Note: If you want it a bit creamier, spread mayonnaise on the inside top bun before topping.**

**1.** Bring the griddle to medium heat.

**2.** While the griddle is coming up to temperature, spread mayonnaise on the inside of each of the buns and place them on the griddle facedown. Once the buns are toasted to a light golden brown, pull and set aside.

**3.** Once the griddle is to temperature, pour the oil on the griddle.

**4.** Place the 4 chicken meatballs in the oil, ensuring space between the meatballs to give them room to be smashed. Sprinkle the Usual Suspects Seasoning liberally on the meatballs.

**5.** After about 30 seconds, smash each meatball all the way down flat with a burger smasher or the back side of the spatula, using the back side of another spatula to help apply pressure. Hold the smash down for 10 to 15 seconds.

**6.** Once each burger is smashed, use the spatula and quickly flip them and place a slice of Swiss cheese on each burger.

**7.** Pull each burger from the heat.

**8.** Place the burgers, stacking one on top of the other, and place on the bottom buns.

**9.** Place the ham on the griddle for about 45 seconds to get hot.

**10.** Pull the ham and place on the burgers. Put a swirl of honey mustard on top of the ham and place the top bun.

# NASHVILLE HOT CHICKEN SMASH BURGER

**YIELD:** 2 burgers

**This refreshing burger is packed with flavor and zest, making it perfect for anyone who like their chicken sandwiches with a spicy kick.**

### NASHVILLE HOT SAUCE

2 tablespoons (10 g) cayenne pepper

1½ tablespoons (23 g) brown sugar (or a bit more for added sweetness)

½ teaspoon chili powder

½ teaspoon garlic powder

½ cup (120 ml) vegetable oil

### BURGERS

1 tablespoon (14 g) mayonnaise, plus additional for topping

2 potato hamburger buns

1 tablespoon (15 ml) vegetable oil

12 ounces (340 g) ground chicken, divided into four 3-ounce (85 g) loosely packed meatballs

4 teaspoons (14 g) Usual Suspects Seasoning (page 92)

1 recipe Nashville Hot Sauce (see above)

8 dill pickle chips

**1.** To make the Nashville hot sauce: Mix all the ingredients together and set aside in a shallow bowl.

**2.** To make the burgers: Bring the griddle to medium heat.

**3.** While the griddle is coming up to temperature, spread mayonnaise on the inside of each of the buns and place them on the griddle facedown. Once the buns are toasted to a light golden brown, pull and set aside.

**4.** Once the griddle is to temperature, pour the oil on the griddle.

**5.** Place the 4 chicken meatballs in the oil, ensuring space between the meatballs to give them room to be smashed. Sprinkle the Usual Suspects Seasoning liberally on the meatballs.

**6.** After about 30 seconds, smash each meatball all the way down flat with a burger smasher or the back side of the spatula, using the back side of another spatula to help apply pressure. Hold the smash down for 10 to 15 seconds.

**7.** Once each burger is smashed, use the spatula and quickly flip them.

**8.** Pull each burger from the heat and submerge in the Nashville Hot Sauce.

**9.** After a dunk in the Nashville Hot Sauce, place the burgers, stacking one on top of the other, on the bottom buns. Top with 4 dill pickle chips. Add a swirl of mayonnaise on the inside of the top buns and place on top of the burgers.

1 tablespoon (15 ml) vegetable oil

12 ounces (340 g) ground chicken, divided into four 3-ounce (85 g) loosely packed meatballs

1 to 1½ teaspoons salt, divided

1 to 1½ teaspoons freshly ground black pepper, divided

4 slices Swiss cheese

2 ciabatta rolls, split in half

1 to 2 Roma tomatoes, sliced

4 slices cooked bacon

¼ cup (60 g) ranch dressing

# CHICKEN BACON RANCH PRESSED SMASH BURGER

**YIELD:** 2 burgers

**Do you ever find yourself craving something savory but also bright and fresh? This perfect chicken smash burger that is exceptionally satisfying to the last bite! Note: A heavy cast iron or other large grill/griddle press is best suited for use with this sandwich.**

**1.** Bring the griddle to medium-high/high heat. Once the griddle is to temperature, pour the oil on the griddle.

**2.** Place the 4 meatballs in the oil, ensuring space between the meatballs to give them room to be smashed. Sprinkle salt and pepper liberally on the meatballs.

**3.** After about 30 seconds, smash each meatball all the way down flat with a burger smasher or the back side of the spatula, using the back side of another spatula to help apply pressure. Hold the smash down for 10 to 15 seconds.

**4.** Once each burger is smashed, use the spatula and quickly flip them and place a slice of Swiss cheese on each burger.

**5.** Pull each burger from the heat.

**6.** Place the burgers, stacking one on top of the other, on the bottom rolls. Build in the following order: bottom roll, smash chicken burgers, tomatoes, sprinkled with ½ teaspoon each of salt and pepper, bacon, a drizzle of ranch dressing, top roll. Place a grill/griddle press on top of the sandwich for about 1 minute. Once the bottom roll is lightly browned, carefully flip the burger and press, being careful not to split the roll. Once the top roll is lightly browned, carefully flip back over and pull from the heat.

# BUFFALO CHICKEN SMASH BURGER

**YIELD:** 2 burgers

**This chicken smash burger version takes your beloved wings and transforms them into a creative option for a delicious dinner, or for a hearty lunch, or maybe even . . . for an eye-opening breakfast? Go ahead. No judgment here.**

1 tablespoon (14 g) mayonnaise, plus an additional ½ tablespoon (7 g) for topping

2 potato hamburger buns

1 tablespoon (15 ml) vegetable oil

12 ounces (340 g) ground chicken, divided into four 3-ounce (85 g) loosely packed meatballs

4 teaspoons (14 g) Usual Suspects Seasoning (page 92)

4 slices provolone cheese

8 dill pickle chips

2 tablespoons (28 ml) buffalo sauce (such as Frank's RedHot Buffalo Wing Sauce)

½ cup (115 g) shredded lettuce

1 tomato, sliced

½ red onion, thinly sliced

2 tablespoons (30 g) ranch dressing, or blue cheese dressing

**1.** Bring the griddle to medium heat.

**2.** While the griddle is coming up to temperature, spread mayonnaise on the inside of each of the buns and place them on the griddle facedown. Once the buns are toasted to a light golden brown, pull and set aside.

**3.** Once the griddle is to temperature, pour the oil on the griddle.

**4.** Place the 4 chicken meatballs in the oil, ensuring space between the meatballs to give them room to be smashed. Sprinkle the Usual Suspects Seasoning liberally on the meatballs.

**5.** After about 30 seconds, smash each meatball all the way down flat with a burger smasher or the back side of the spatula, using the back side of another spatula to help apply pressure. Hold the smash down for 10 to 15 seconds.

**6.** Once each burger is smashed, use the spatula and quickly flip them and place a slice of provolone cheese on each burger.

**7.** Pull each burger from the heat.

**8.** Place the burgers, stacking one on top of the other, on the bottom buns. Build in the following order: bottom bun, swirl of mayonnaise, 4 pickle chips, smash chicken burgers, buffalo sauce, lettuce, tomato, onion, ranch dressing, top bun.

5

# MAIN COURSES

# CHEESY CHICKEN PIZZAIOLA

**YIELD:** 6 to 8 servings

**This recipe very well could become your new family favorite. The seasoning makes about ¼ cup (50 g) for a shaker and will keep, stored in a cool, dry place, for up to 6 months.**

### USUAL SUSPECTS SEASONING

1 tablespoon (18 g) salt

1 tablespoon (10 g) garlic powder

1 tablespoon (12 g) Ac'cent Flavor Enhancer

1½ teaspoons freshly ground black pepper

1½ teaspoons onion powder

1½ teaspoons adobo seasoning

### CHEESY CHICKEN PIZZAIOLA

1 (24-ounce [70 ml]) jar marinara sauce

1 (16-ounce [454 g]) package penne pasta

1 to 2 tablespoons (15 to 30 ml) vegetable or olive oil

4 boneless, skinless chicken breasts, pounded thin

4 ounces (115 g) thinly sliced deli ham, or enough to cover each chicken breast with 2 or 3 slices

Shredded mozzarella cheese for topping

---

**1.** To make the Usual Suspects Seasoning: In a small bowl, stir together all the Usual Suspects ingredients, then transfer to a shaker.

**2.** To make the chicken pizzaiola: In a small saucepan over medium heat, warm the marinara sauce. Keep warm until serving.

**3.** While the sauce warms, bring a large pot of water to a boil. Add the pasta and cook according to the package instructions. Drain and set aside while you prepare the main dish.

**4.** Preheat the griddle to medium-low heat.

**5.** Coat the hot griddle with oil, place the chicken on it, and season liberally with Usual Suspects Seasoning. Cook for 3 to 4 minutes, flip the chicken, and cook for 3 to 4 minutes more. Continue cooking and flipping until the internal temperature of the chicken reaches a minimum of 165°F (74°C), 8 to 10 minutes total. Move the chicken to the cooler side of the griddle, not over direct heat.

**6.** Place the ham slices on the griddle and cook for 20 to 30 seconds, just long enough to get them hot. Pull the ham off the griddle.

**7.** Place the pasta and three-fourths of the sauce in a large serving dish. Toss to coat.

**8.** Turn the griddle to low heat and move the chicken over direct heat. Top each piece with a generous spoonful of the remaining sauce, then with two or three slices of ham. Sprinkle with mozzarella to taste. Dome the chicken to melt the cheese. Transfer the chicken to the serving dish with the pasta and sauce. If you like it saucy, spread the remaining sauce over the entire dish before serving.

# CHICKEN STREET TACOS WITH CREAMY JALAPEÑO RANCH

**YIELD:** 4 to 6 servings

**Take Taco Tuesday to the next level with these amazing chicken street tacos. This one will have your family coming over for more week after week.**

### CREAMY JALAPEÑO RANCH

1 (1-ounce [28 g]) packet ranch dressing mix

1 cup (240 ml) milk

1 cup (240 g) mayonnaise

1 or 2 medium-size jalapeño peppers, seeded and finely chopped

2 tablespoons (2 g) finely chopped fresh cilantro

1 to 2 tablespoons (15 to 30 ml) freshly squeezed lime juice

1 to 2 teaspoons dill pickle brine

### CHICKEN STREET TACOS

2 tablespoons (24 g) Tajín seasoning

1 tablespoon (12 g) Usual Suspects Seasoning (page 92)

2 pounds (908 g) boneless, skinless chicken thighs

2 tablespoons (30 ml) vegetable oil

3 limes, halved

8 to 10 (4½-inch [11 cm]) street-size taco flour tortillas

1 cup (115 g) shredded Mexican-style cheese blend

½ cup (8 g) chopped fresh cilantro

**1.** To make the creamy jalapeño ranch: In a medium-size bowl, whisk all the dressing ingredients well. Cover and refrigerate for at least 30 minutes before serving.

**2.** To make the street tacos: In a small bowl, stir together the Tajín seasoning and Usual Suspects Seasoning. Set aside.

**3.** Pound the chicken thighs out as flat as possible, about ⅛ to ¼ inch (0.3 to 0.6 cm) thick, without breaking or tearing the meat.

**4.** Bring the griddle to medium-low heat.

**5.** Pour the oil onto the griddle and place the chicken thighs in the oil. Cook for 2 to 3 minutes, or until the chicken is about halfway cooked (light brown in color). Season the top of the chicken thighs liberally with about half of the Tajín mixture and squeeze two lime halves over the chicken. Flip the chicken thighs and season them with the remaining Tajín mixture. Squeeze two more lime halves over the chicken and cook for 2 minutes, or until the internal temperature reaches at least 165°F (74°C). Pull the chicken off the griddle and let it rest for 5 minutes. Cut the chicken meat into ¼-inch (0.6 cm) strips.

**6.** Place the tortillas onto a clean area of the warm griddle for about 30 seconds. On each tortilla, place a small handful of shredded cheese, four or five strips of chicken, a drizzle of jalapeño ranch, and cilantro to taste. Serve with the remaining lime halves for squeezing.

# HAWAIIAN BARBECUE CHICKEN

**YIELD:** Serves 8

**This easy recipe is a fast adaptation for that island flair when you don't have access to all the island-favorite ingredients! Serve with Hawaiian Macaroni Salad (page 45) for the complete experience.**

3 cups (720 ml) soy sauce

1 cup (200 g) sugar

1 cup (240 ml) water

½ teaspoon minced peeled fresh ginger

¼ teaspoon minced garlic

¼ teaspoon freshly ground black pepper

4 pounds (1.8 kg) boneless, skinless chicken thighs

2 to 3 tablespoons (30 to 45 ml) vegetable oil

**1.** In a large bowl, whisk the soy sauce, sugar, water, ginger, garlic, and pepper to blend. Add the chicken, turning it to coat in the marinade. Cover and refrigerate for at least 5 hours.

**2.** When ready to cook, bring the griddle to medium-low heat.

**3.** Pour the oil onto the griddle and let it heat until you see a wisp of white smoke. Remove the chicken from the marinade and lay it in the hot oil. Discard the marinade. Cook for 3 to 4 minutes, checking to ensure the chicken is not burning. (It will darken, and some spots may look burned, but it is the caramelization of the marinade.) Flip the chicken to cook the other side for 3 minutes. Flip the chicken a final time and cook until the internal temperature is at least 165°F (74°C). Pull the chicken from the grill and serve.

# CHICKEN CORDON BLEU

**YIELD:** 2 servings

**This griddle-fried chicken cordon bleu is a timeless favorite that brings a touch of French-inspired flair to your dinner table.**

2 boneless skinless, chicken breasts

3 to 4 teaspoons (12 to 16 g) Usual Suspects Seasoning (page 92), plus more for the dredge

2 tablespoons (30 g) honey mustard

8 slices Swiss cheese

2 slices deli ham

1 to 2 cups (120 to 240 g) all-purpose flour

1 cup (240 ml) buttermilk

½ cup (25 g) panko breadcrumbs

**1.** Bring the griddle to medium heat.

**2.** While the griddle heats, butterfly the chicken by cutting through the middle of each breast horizontally, but do not cut all the way through the other side. Open the breasts like a book. Pound the chicken breasts to ¼-inch (0.6 cm) thickness. Season each piece of chicken on both sides with the Usual Suspects Seasoning.

**3.** Spread the honey mustard liberally, to taste, over the inside (the rough side) of the chicken. Place two cheese slices and one ham slice on one side of each breast, then top that with two more cheese slices. Fold each breast over to enclose the ham and cheese.

**4.** Place the flour in a shallow bowl and season it to taste with the Usual Suspects Seasoning. Whisk with a fork to blend. Pour the buttermilk into another shallow bowl and put the breadcrumbs in a third bowl. Dredge each breast in the flour, ensuring the entire surface (both sides) is completely coated and, being careful to keep the bundle together, submerge both sides in the buttermilk and place the chicken into the breadcrumbs, ensuring complete coverage.

**5.** Put the chicken on the griddle and cook for 5 minutes, then carefully flip. Continue to cook and flip the chicken until it is no longer pink and the internal temperature reaches 165°F (74°C).

# BOURBON CHICKEN

**YIELD:** 4 to 6 servings

**Does bourbon chicken really need bourbon to be considered bourbon chicken? Nope! In fact, this dish carries a common misconception due to its name, which was derived from where it was created: Bourbon Street in New Orleans. With or without bourbon, this dish delivers amazing flavor in every bite. Serve with your favorite side dish.**

- 1⁄3 cup (75 g) packed brown sugar
- 1⁄3 cup (80 ml) soy sauce
- 1⁄4 cup (60 ml) apple juice
- 2 tablespoons (30 ml) olive oil
- 2 tablespoons (30 g) ketchup
- 1 tablespoon (15 ml) apple cider vinegar
- 1 garlic clove, minced
- 1⁄4 teaspoon ground ginger
- 3⁄4 teaspoon red pepper flakes
- 2 pounds (908 g) boneless, skinless chicken breast, cut into 1⁄2-inch (1 cm) pieces
- 1⁄2 cup (120 ml) water plus 2 tablespoons (30 ml)
- 1 tablespoon (8 g) cornstarch

**1.** Bring one side of the griddle to high heat and the other side to medium-low heat.

**2.** In a medium-size skillet over high heat, stir together the brown sugar, soy sauce, apple juice, oil, ketchup, vinegar, garlic, ginger, and red pepper flakes. Bring to a boil. (On the griddle, this will take longer than on the stovetop; to speed up the process, cook the sauce on the stovetop.)

**3.** While the sauce heats, place the chicken on the griddle over medium-low heat. Cook, turning occasionally, until the chicken is light brown and nearly cooked through.

**4.** Once the sauce comes to a rolling boil, in a small bowl, whisk the water and cornstarch until the cornstarch dissolves. Whisk this slurry into the sauce. Return the sauce to a boil, reduce the heat to medium, and cook until it reaches your desired thickness.

**5.** Pour the sauce over the chicken on the griddle, cooking, mixing, and stirring, until the chicken is thoroughly cooked and no longer pink and the sauce coats the chicken nicely.

#### SASSY SAUCE

1 cup (240 g) ketchup

2 teaspoons water, plus more as needed

1 teaspoon garlic powder, plus more as needed

#### FAMOUS BEEF 'N' CHEDDAR COPYCAT

2 tablespoons (28 g) unsalted butter

2 tablespoons (15 g) all-purpose flour

2 cups (480 ml) whole milk

2 cups (230 g) shredded cheddar cheese

Shredded American cheese for the sauce

1 to 2 teaspoons salt

1 pound (454 g) thinly sliced deli roast beef

4 onion buns

# FAMOUS BEEF 'N' CHEDDAR COPYCAT WITH SASSY SAUCE

**YIELD:** 4 to 6 servings

**Craving that iconic beef and cheddar sandwich but want to make it at home with a little extra flair? This copycat recipe delivers roast beef, melty cheddar, and a sassy sauce that steals the show.**

**1.** To make the sassy sauce: In a small bowl, stir together the ketchup, water, and garlic powder until blended. Taste and adjust as needed.

**2.** To make the cheddar sauce: In a medium-size saucepan, on the stovetop or griddle over medium-high heat, melt the butter. Stir in the flour to create a roux (a cooked mixture of flour and fat used as a thickener in a soup or a sauce). As soon as the flour is incorporated into the butter, stirring constantly, pour in the milk a little at a time. As the roux thickens, add more milk, stirring, until all the milk is incorporated. Add the cheddar and mix until the cheese is completely melted. Stir in the American cheese to taste and salt (begin with 1 teaspoon) until you like how the sauce tastes. Keep warm (the cheese sauce will begin to solidify when cooling; to reuse, gently reheat the cheese sauce).

**3.** Bring a separate area of the griddle to medium-low heat. Place the roast beef slices on the griddle and cook for about 1 minute per side, just long enough to get the meat hot. Pull the meat from the heat. Place the buns, cut-side down, on the griddle for about 1 minute, or until the inside is lightly toasted.

**4.** To build the sandwich: Spread a spoonful of sassy sauce on the bottom bun. Stack the roast beef about an inch (2.5 cm) thick on the bottom bun and add a generous drizzle of cheese sauce. Spread another spoonful of sauce on the inside of the top bun and place the bun on the sandwich.

# TRADITIONAL PHILLY CHEESESTEAKS

**YIELD:** 4 servings

**Nothing beats the authentic Philly cheesesteak—a perfect marriage of thinly sliced, tender steak and melted cheese, all piled high in a soft, crusty hoagie roll.**

**These simple yet delicious ingredients create a sub that's beloved for its rich flavor and satisfying bite. Add sauteed peppers or mushrooms to beef this recipe up.**

3 tablespoons (45 ml) vegetable oil, divided

3 tablespoons (42 g) unsalted butter

1 large yellow onion, diced

Salt and freshly ground black pepper

1 pound (454 g) rib eye, shaved or sliced as thinly as possible

12 slices provolone cheese

4 hoagie rolls, split horizontally

**1.** Bring the griddle to medium-low heat.

**2.** Pour 1 tablespoon (15 ml) of oil onto the griddle, then add the butter to melt. Lay the onion in the melted butter and season with 1 teaspoon of salt and 1 teaspoon of pepper. Cook for 5 to 6 minutes, moving the onion slowly, until it begins to turn translucent. Move the onion to a cooler side of the griddle, not over direct heat, or take it off the griddle.

**3.** Pour the remaining 2 tablespoons (30 ml) of oil onto the griddle and lay the rib eye in the oil, spreading it out. Season with salt and pepper to taste. Cook the rib eye, spread out and flat, on the griddle for 1 to 2 minutes to create a sear. Once the meat begins to turn brown, indicating it is cooking through, stir and "chop" the rib eye with a scraper to break up the meat. Mix in the onion, then divide the meat and onion into four even lines, each the length of a hoagie roll. Lay three slices of cheese on each line of meat to melt.

**4.** Place the hoagie rolls on the griddle for about 1 minute to warm the outside of each roll. Open each roll and place one facedown on each line of cheesesteak and let sit for about 30 seconds. Using a spatula, scoop up the cheesesteak, holding firm to the hoagie, and turn the whole sandwich right-side up.

Jasmine rice for serving

⅓ cup (80 ml) soy sauce

2½ tablespoons (38 g) brown sugar

2 tablespoons (30 ml) sesame oil

1 tablespoon (8 g) grated peeled fresh ginger

3 garlic cloves, minced

1 bunch scallions, white and green parts, chopped, separated

1½ pounds (681 g) New York strip steak or sirloin

1½ teaspoons vegetable oil

# KOREAN-STYLE BARBECUE BEEF (BULGOGI)

**YIELD:** 4 to 6 servings

**This salty, sweet, spicy from the ginger, restaurant-level cook, made at home on your griddle, is a crowd-pleaser. Add your favorite Korean sides, like kimchi, spicy cucumber salad, pickled onions, or pancakes, to complete the meal.**

**1.** Prepare as much rice as you need for serving according to the package instructions. Keep warm until needed.

**2.** In a medium-size bowl, whisk the soy sauce, brown sugar, sesame oil, ginger, garlic, and scallion whites to combine. Set aside.

**3.** Cut the steak into very thin strips and place them in a large resealable plastic bag. Pour in the soy marinade, seal the bag, and turn the steak to coat, ensuring it's covered in the marinade. Refrigerate for at least 1 hour.

**4.** Bring the griddle to medium-low heat.

**5.** Pour the vegetable oil onto the griddle. Remove the beef from the marinade and place it in the oil. Discard the marinade. Cook for 1 minute to sear the steak. Flip the steak and cook for 1 minute more. Pull the beef off the griddle and serve over the jasmine rice, garnished with the scallion greens.

# MONGOLIAN-STYLE BEEF

**YIELD:** 4 servings

**Mongolian-Style Beef blends sweet, savory, and a bit of spice. You can serve this over rice or noodles for a satisfying meal.**

2 New York strip steaks (about 1½ pounds [681 g] total), thinly sliced

3 tablespoons (24 g) cornstarch

3 tablespoons (45 ml) vegetable oil, divided, plus more as needed

3 garlic cloves, minced

1 tablespoon (6 g) minced peeled fresh ginger

⅓ cup (80 ml) soy sauce

⅓ cup (80 ml) water

½ cup (113 g) packed brown sugar

Steamed rice for serving (preferably jasmine)

2 scallions, white and green parts, cut into 1-inch (2.5 cm) pieces

1 teaspoon toasted sesame seeds (optional)

**1.** Cut the sirloin into ⅛-inch (0.3 cm)-thick strips. Place them in a medium-size bowl, add the cornstarch, and mix well to evenly coat all of the steak.

**2.** Bring the griddle to medium-high heat.

**3.** Place a small saucepan over the heat and pour in 1 tablespoon (15 ml) of oil to heat. Add the garlic and ginger and sauté for about 1 minute—do not let the garlic brown. Add the soy sauce, water, and brown sugar. Cook, stirring, until the sauce comes to a rolling boil and the sugar dissolves.

**4.** While the sauce cooks, bring another section of the griddle to medium heat.

**5.** Pour 1 to 2 tablespoons (15 to 30 ml) of oil onto the griddle over medium heat and place the steak in the oil. Sear the first side for about 30 seconds. Flip the steak and cook for 1 minute. Pour the sauce over the steak and cook until the sauce thickens on the steak. Pull the steak off the griddle and serve over rice, garnished with scallions and sesame seeds (if using).

2 pounds (908 g) stir-fry beef

5 tablespoons (75 ml) sweet soy sauce, divided

3 tablespoons (45 ml) vegetable oil, divided

2 teaspoons salt

1 teaspoon freshly ground black pepper

4 large eggs

1 (12-ounce [340 g]) bag frozen vegetable stir-fry mix

# BEEF STIR-FRY ON THE GRIDDLE

**YIELD:** 6 to 8 servings

**In the mood for amazing Asian cuisine? Look no further. This beef stir-fry will satisfy any craving. Marinating the meat the night before makes this one of the quickest cooks on the griddle! Look for sweet soy sauce at Asian markets. Serve with your favorite sides.**

**1.** In a shallow dish, combine the beef and 2 tablespoons (30 ml) of sweet soy sauce. Toss to coat well. Cover and refrigerate overnight.

**2.** Bring the griddle to medium-low heat.

**3.** Pour about 2 tablespoons (30 ml) of oil onto the griddle, then place the beef on it. Cook the beef until about halfway cooked through (some pink remains), then cover the beef with 2 tablespoons (30 ml) of sweet soy sauce and season with salt and pepper. Stir-fry the beef in the sauce for 2 to 3 minutes, then pull the beef to the cooler side of the griddle, not over direct heat.

**4.** Pour another 1 tablespoon (15 ml) of oil onto the griddle again. Crack the eggs into the oil and cook, scrambling, until almost cooked through, flip the eggs, and cook until fully cooked. Place the eggs on the beef.

**5.** Place the vegetables on the griddle (preheat the vegetables in the microwave to make the cooking process quicker) and stir-fry for about 2 minutes, or until the vegetables are hot and cooked through. Pull the beef and eggs back onto the heat and mix all the ingredients together. Top everything with the remaining 1 tablespoon (15 ml) of sweet soy sauce and cook for 1 to 2 minutes before pulling off the griddle to serve.

# CHEESESTEAK QUESADILLAS

**YIELD:** 4 to 6 servings

**Shaved rib eye can serve many purposes—especially in the form of a "cheesesteak!" It might be hard to pick your favorite way to serve shaved beef: the hoagie, the tortilla, the egg roll . . . but these quesadillas are tough to beat.**

**1.** Bring the griddle to medium-low heat.

**2.** Pour 1 tablespoon (15 ml) of oil onto the griddle, then place the butter on it to melt. Lay the onion in the melted butter, followed by the green pepper, and add 1 teaspoon of salt and 1 teaspoon of pepper. Cook for 5 to 6 minutes, moving the vegetables slowly, until the onion begins to turn translucent. Move the vegetables to a cooler side of the griddle, not over direct heat, or set aside off the griddle.

**3.** Pour the remaining 2 tablespoons (30 ml) of oil onto the griddle and lay the rib eye flat in it, spreading it out. Season with the remaining 1 teaspoon of salt and 1 teaspoon of pepper. Cook for 1 to 2 minutes to create a sear. Once the meat begins to turn brown, indicating it is cooked through, stir and chop the rib eye with a scraper to break up the meat. Mix the cooked rib eye with the onion and pepper and set aside.

**4.** Clean a space on the griddle to cook the quesadillas. Spread butter on one side of each tortilla. Lay four tortillas on the griddle and build each quesadilla by laying a generous amount of the steak and vegetables onto the tortilla (ensuring equal parts for all quesadillas). Place three slices of provolone over the rib eye on each and place a second tortilla on top, butter-side up. Cook the quesadillas until the bottom tortilla is golden brown, carefully flip the tortilla with a spatula, and continue cooking until the cheese is melted and the bottom tortilla is golden brown. Pull the tortillas from the heat and cut into quarters to serve with your favorite dipping sauce.

3 tablespoons (45 ml) vegetable oil, divided

2 tablespoons (28 g) unsalted butter, plus more for the tortillas

1 large yellow onion, diced

1 green bell pepper, diced

2 teaspoons salt, divided

2 teaspoons freshly ground black pepper, divided

1 pound (454 g) rib eye, shaved or as thinly sliced as possible

8 (6-inch [15 cm]) taco-size flour tortillas

12 slices provolone cheese

Favorite dipping sauce for serving

# GRILLED CHEESE BURRITOS

**YIELD:** 6 to 8 servings

**Imagine pairing your favorite cheese with rice, ground beef, and seasonings. How could you pass on that? Add in your favorite toppings to make this burrito your own.**

1 (5.6-ounce [159 g]) package Spanish or Mexican rice

2 tablespoons (30 ml) vegetable oil

1 pound (454 g) 80/20 ground beef

1 (1-ounce [28 g]) packet taco seasoning

6 to 8 (10-inch [25 cm]) burrito-size flour tortillas

1 (15-ounce [425 g]) jar cheese sauce/queso dip

1 to 2 pounds (454 to 908 g) shredded cheese of choice

Sour cream for serving

1 large tomato, sliced

**1.** Cook the rice according to the package directions. Keep warm.

**2.** Bring the griddle to medium-low heat.

**3.** Pour the oil onto the griddle and place the ground beef in it. Cook for 4 to 5 minutes, breaking up the meat, until brown. Season the beef with the taco seasoning, cook for 3 to 4 minutes, mixing it in, then pull the ground beef off the heat.

**4.** Place the tortillas on the griddle for 30 seconds to 1 minute to warm. Once warmed, transfer to a work surface and build the burritos: Spread the tortillas with a layer of queso dip, followed by ground beef, cheese, a few dollops of sour cream, rice, and tomato slices. Fold in the sides and firmly roll up the burritos.

**5.** On a cleared area of the griddle, lay down a strip of shredded cheese, the length of a burrito, and place the first burrito directly onto the cheese. Cook for about 1 minute, or until the cheese is melted onto the tortilla. Create a second strip of cheese on the griddle in front of the burrito. Using a scraper or sturdy spatula, flip the burrito so the top side is now resting on the second layer of cheese. Cook for about 1 minute until the cheese melts onto the burrito. Pull and place on a plate for serving. Repeat with the remaining burritos and shredded cheese.

# GLAZED PORK BELLY

**YIELD:** 4 to 6 servings

**Seemingly inconspicuous, this pork belly and glaze cook has outstanding flavor. You'll be talking about this one for days.**

¼ cup (80 g) honey

¼ cup (60 ml) soy sauce

2 tablespoons (30 ml) oyster sauce

2 teaspoons minced garlic

2 pounds (908 g) pork belly, cut into ¼-to ½-inch (0.6 to 1 cm)-thick slices

Salt

**1.** In a small bowl, stir together the honey, soy sauce, oyster sauce, and garlic until blended.

**2.** Bring the griddle to medium-low heat.

**3.** Place the pork belly slices on the griddle and season liberally with salt. Cook for 2 to 3 minutes until the pork begins to brown. Turn each piece, season with salt, and cook for 2 to 3 minutes more to brown. Continue cooking and flipping until each piece is browned and cooked as desired.

**4.** Brush the pork with the glaze. Flip the pork belly and brush the other side with glaze. Cook for 2 to 3 minutes to help the glaze caramelize—but not burn! Pull the pork off the griddle and serve.

# SHRIMP STIR-FRY

**YIELD:** 4 servings

**Need an excuse to make another mouthwatering Asian-inspired dish, or just another shrimp recipe? Say no more. Serve with your favorite sides for a complete meal.**

### STIR-FRY SAUCE

1 cup (240 ml) chicken broth

¼ cup (62.5 g) hoisin sauce

2 tablespoons (30 ml) soy sauce

2 teaspoons sesame oil

1 tablespoon (8 g) cornstarch

### SHRIMP STIR-FRY

2 tablespoons (30 ml) vegetable oil, divided

1 red bell pepper, cut into 2-inch (5 cm) slices

1 yellow bell pepper, cut into 2-inch (5 cm) slices

1 orange bell pepper, cut into 2-inch (5 cm) slices

½ yellow onion, cut into 2-inch (5 cm) strips

3 cups (210 g) broccoli florets

1 to 2 tablespoons (14 to 28 g) unsalted butter

Salt and freshly ground black pepper

1½ teaspoons garlic paste

1 teaspoon ginger paste

1 pound (454 g) medium-size shrimp, peeled and deveined

Sliced scallion for garnish

Sesame seeds for garnish

**1.** To make the stir-fry sauce: In a medium-size bowl, whisk all the sauce ingredients until combined. Set aside.

**2.** Bring the griddle to medium-low heat.

**3.** To make the shrimp stir-fry: Pour 1 tablespoon (15 ml) of vegetable oil onto the griddle and place the bell peppers, onion, and broccoli in the oil. Add the butter and incorporate it into the vegetables. Season the vegetables with salt and pepper. Cook the vegetables for about 10 minutes, slowly mixing, or until the onion becomes translucent.

**4.** On another part of the griddle, combine 1 tablespoon (15 ml) of oil, the garlic paste, and ginger paste and mix to combine and cook until the garlic begins to brown (do not wait too long or the garlic will burn). Place the shrimp on the garlic-ginger mixture and cook, stirring, for 3 to 4 minutes, or until the shrimp are pink and opaque.

**5.** Mix the cooked shrimp with the vegetables. Pour in the stir-fry sauce a little at a time, using as much or as little sauce as you like. Serve garnished with the scallion and sesame seeds.

# BANG BANG SHRIMP

**YIELD:** 2 servings

**Bang Bang Shrimp is the kind of meal that disappears in minutes. Lightly battered shrimp are fried to golden perfection, then tossed in a bold, tangy-sweet chili mayo sauce that delivers a serious flavor punch. Serve this as a standalone meal or add the shrimp to tacos or a rice bowl.**

1 cup (240 g) mayonnaise

¾ cup (237 g) sweet chili sauce (Use liberally!)

2 teaspoons sriracha, plus more as needed

4 large eggs, beaten

3 to 4 cups (360 to 480 g) all-purpose flour

2 tablespoons (16 g) cornstarch

1 pound (454 g) shrimp, peeled and deveined

2 to 3 tablespoons (30 to 45 ml) vegetable oil, divided

**1.** In a large bowl, stir together the mayo, chili sauce, and sriracha until blended. Taste and add more sriracha, as needed. Set aside.

**2.** Place two shallow bowls side by side. Place the eggs in one bowl and stir together the flour and cornstarch in the other. Pat the shrimp dry with a paper towel. Coat the shrimp in the egg wash, then move it to the flour mixture to coat.

**3.** Bring the griddle to medium-low heat.

**4.** Pour the oil onto the griddle and let heat until you see a wisp of white smoke. Place the coated shrimp on the griddle in the hot oil. Cook the shrimp for 1 minute, or until the bottom is browned, turn, and repeat on the other side, adding more oil as needed. Transfer the cooked shrimp to the bowl with the sauce and stir to coat it evenly.

2 fresh tuna steaks

2 tablespoons (30 ml) soy sauce

1½ teaspoons sesame oil

1 to 2 tablespoons (8 to 16 g) black and white sesame seeds, mixed

2 tablespoons (30 ml) olive oil

# SEARED AHI TUNA

**YIELD:** 2 servings

**This dish celebrates the natural richness of the tuna while adding just enough seasoning for contrast. If you need the ultimate savory yet light meal, this one delivers!**

**1.** Pat the tuna steaks completely dry with a paper towel. In a small bowl or on a small plate, stir together the soy sauce and sesame oil. Pour the sesame seeds onto another small plate. Place the tuna in the soy–sesame oil mixture and ensure it is completely coated. Then lay it in the sesame seeds and press lightly to help cover the entire backside of the tuna with seeds. Flip and do the same to the other side. Roll the sides in the seeds to completely cover the tuna in sesame seeds.

**2.** Bring the griddle to high heat.

**3.** Pour the olive oil onto the griddle and place the tuna in the oil. Cook for 1 minute per side. Pull the tuna off the griddle and let rest for 5 to 10 minutes before serving. Cut the tuna against the grain into slices to serve.

# INDEX

# ALSO AVAILABLE

**Smoking**
978-0-7603-9745-9

**Grilling**
978-0-7603-9747-3

**Camp Cooking**
978-1-57715-656-7

**Rice Cooker**
978-0-7603-9741-1

**Slow Cooker**
978-1-57715-658-1

**Bread Machine**
978-1-57715-660-4

**Air Fryer**
978-0-7603-9743-5